PAULA ABDUL STRAIGHT UP

PAULA ABDUL

STRAIGHT UP

M. Thomas Ford

DILLON PRESS
New York

Maxwell Macmillan Canada
Toronto

Maxwell Macmillan International
New York   Oxford   Singapore   Sydney

Photographic Acknowledgments

Front and back covers: AP—Wide World Photos

Retna Pictures, Ltd.: Kees Tabak (5): Frank Micelotta (6, 62); Tammie Arroya (10); Steve Granitz (24, 36, 40, 50, 54, 66); Ken Berard (33, 46); Scott Weiner (49); Gary Gershoff (57); Hollis (65)

Ron Galella, Ltd.: Jim Smeal (13, 16, 53, 59); Randy Bauer (43)

Van Nuys High *Crimson and Gray*, 1980: (19, 21)

Wen Roberts/Photography Ink: (27, 30)

Library of Congress Cataloging-in-Publication Data

Ford, M. Thomas.
    Paula Abdul : straight up / M. Thomas Ford.
        p. cm. — (Taking part)
    Discography: p.
    Summary: A biography of the entertainer whose energetic choreography changed the look of cheerleading and rock videos and led to her multifaceted career.
    ISBN 0-87518-508-8
    1. Abdul, Paula—Juvenile literature. 2. Singers—United States—Biography—Juvenile literature. 3. Dancers—United States—Biography—Juvenile literature. 4. Choreographers—United States—Biography—Juvenile literature. [1. Abdul, Paula. 2. Entertainers.] I. Title. II. Series.
ML3930.A25F7 1992
782.42166'092—dc20   91-40231
[B]

Dillon Press
Macmillan Publishing Company
866 Third Avenue
New York, NY 10022

Maxwell Macmillan Canada, Inc.
1200 Eglinton Avenue East
Suite 200
Don Mills, Ontario M3C 3N1

Macmillan Publishing Company is part of the Maxwell Communication Group of Companies.

First edition

Printed in the United States of America

10 9 8 7 6 5 4 3 2 1

CONTENTS

INTRODUCTION:

"I'm in a funky way!"

The stage is dark. Behind a thin curtain shadows are moving silently. Every so often the sound of a guitar being tuned or a microphone being tested is heard. The people in the audience wait anxiously to see what will happen next.

Then it grows quiet. The curtains open a little bit and a very tall figure on stilts appears. He is wearing a big top hat and a long black coat. He walks slowly to the center of the stage, bows to the audience, and announces in a booming voice, "Ladies and gentlemen...Paula Abdul!"

There is a roar of excitement from the crowd as light floods the stage and the band launches into a

◀ Paula shows off her new look and sound at the 1991 MTV Music Video Awards.

song. A group of dancers dressed in baggy suits enters from the side of the stage and begins moving to the beat. Suddenly they step back, and right in the middle of them is Paula Abdul, disguised by dark glasses and a fake mustache. "I'm in a funky way!" she yells, and starts singing and dancing her way through "Vibeology," the latest single from her new album.

This is the 1991 MTV Video Music Awards, and people all over the world have tuned in to see and hear Paula Abdul, the hottest performer on the music scene today. For the next seven minutes, Paula shows off her new look and her new sound, leading the dancers through the lightning-quick combination of street moves and classical routines that have made her the most sought-after choreographer around. At one point in the show, the dancers run to the sidelines, leaving Paula alone onstage. "Go, Paula; go, Paula; go, Paula," the band chants, and Paula dazzles the audience with an explosive display of footwork.

When Paula ends her song, the audience applauds wildly, whistling and calling out her name as she leaves the stage. Paula gives them a big smile and waves back to her fans.

Later in the evening, Paula is up for an award for Best Female Video for her work on the video for her song "Rush Rush." The video recently held the number one spot on the video countdown for several weeks, and many people expect her to win.

Paula is up against tough competition—superstar Madonna, newcomer Neneh Cherry, chart sensation Amy Grant, and Paula's old dancing student, Janet Jackson. When the winner is announced, the award goes to Janet Jackson. But even though Paula didn't win this time, she has a lot to be proud of. This was her first live television performance since she finished her new album, and it has gone very well. She is about to launch a major tour, and her new single is rushing up the charts, headed for the number one spot. She's come a long way from being the little girl who used to watch old movies and dream about being a dancing and singing superstar. And she's just beginning!

1

CLASSIC FILMS AND A LITTLE GIRL'S DREAMS

*"Someone once told me her
feet could think."*

—Lorraine Abdul

Today it is hard to listen to the radio, turn on the television, or walk by a newsstand without seeing or hearing Paula Abdul. Her songs and videos are playing constantly, and her picture has been on the cover of almost every magazine around. Since she first burst onto the scene in 1988, she has been a major star. But how did she get to where she is, and who is the person behind this super singer, dancer, and choreographer?

Paula Abdul was born on June 19, 1962. She is the second child of Harry and Lorraine Abdul. Her sister, Wendy, is seven years older than Paula. The Abdul family lived in a quiet suburb in North Hollywood, California. Harry Abdul was in the cattle business.

◀ Ever since she was a little girl, Paula dreamed of being a star.

Lorraine Abdul was for many years the executive assistant to Billy Wilder, the legendary director who made many of the most memorable films of the 1940s and 1950s, including *Sunset Boulevard* and *Some Like It Hot.*

Because of her mother's job, the young Paula got her first taste of the excitement of show business. The little girl would sometimes accompany her mother to the studio lot and would get to see the stars close up. Going into the studio cafeteria for lunch, she might run into celebrities like Debbie Reynolds and John Travolta.

Now that Paula is a star herself, she enjoys making visits back to the set. She says, "What's funny is going back to the studios for meetings. Some of the same guards are there, and they still remember me as Lorraine's daughter."

One of Paula's favorite things to do as a little girl was watch movies. She would sit on the couch in her family's living room and watch classic films on television, dreaming about being a movie star herself one day. Her favorite films were ones that featured dancers

Paula is joined at the 17th Annual American Music Awards by her mother, Lorraine, and her sister, Wendy. ▶

such as Fred Astaire, Ginger Rogers, and, especially, Gene Kelly. She recalls, "When I was a child growing up, I remember when I was four years old sitting on the couch with my parents watching *Singin' in the Rain* on the TV and watching Gene Kelly just have a great time. And I remember being at that age in the living room and saying, 'I want to do that.'" Paula watched the movie over and over, memorizing the dance scenes. "I'd actually dream about being in scenes," she says, "singing and dancing with Gene Kelly."

Paula is very close to her parents, so it was difficult for her when they divorced when she was seven. Paula and Wendy lived with their mother. And even though their father remained in their lives, the separation was hard on the girls. "I saw my dad on weekends," Paula says about this period in her life, "but I missed him a lot."

Despite their age difference, Paula and her sister were very close as children, spending most of their time together. Today they are still best friends. Paula often visits Wendy and her two boys, Alex and Austin, who love to see their famous aunt in person as well as on MTV. Paula credits Wendy with helping to influence her musical tastes. While most of Paula's peers were listening to pop music, Wendy and her friends introduced her to the varied sounds of artists like Stevie Wonder and Carole King.

Paula's career as a dancer began almost by accident at the age of seven. "She was supposed to go to a friend's house," her mother recalls. "The mother called me and said that she forgot her daughter had a dance lesson and wanted to know if she could take Paula."

Paula went along to her friend's dance class and was immediately hooked. When Lorraine picked Paula up the next day, she remembers, "All I heard on the way home was 'I have to take dancing.'"

Wendy was already taking dance lessons at a nearby studio, so Paula started going, too. Her teacher there was Dean Barlow, who taught Paula for many years and is still her adviser on her videos and stage shows. She loved dancing and took to it immediately, practicing all the time. She would practice her steps wherever she happened to be. Sometimes this got her into

trouble. One story, which Paula only laughs about if you ask her about it, is that she once knocked over an entire display of cans in a supermarket while showing off a new move!

Dancing seemed to come naturally to Paula, and soon she was exploring all the different styles. "Dancing—ballet, tap, jazz—was like a reward to me," she says. "A special treat."

Even at the age of seven, Paula's ability and explosive energy were obvious. "Someone once told me her feet could think," her mother says. "She had the ability to see a routine once and get it right away."

If you ask Paula where she got her dancing talent, she says, "My dad—he's Syrian and Brazilian—claims I got my rhythm from him." Whether or not she inherited her talent, Paula did inherit something else from her parents—her height. At a little over five feet tall, she is much shorter than most dancers. While she was growing up, many of her teachers told her that she would probably never work as a professional dancer because she was too short. Today she can look back on

◄ Paula's nephews, Alex and Austin, on the town with their famous aunt at the opening of a Teenage Mutant Ninja Turtles film.

this and laugh, but at the time it really hurt her.

Oddly enough, even though Paula loved dancing, she didn't set out to be a choreographer, something she is very well known for now. She wanted to act and sing. But when she started trying out for acting parts in school shows, she found herself in demand as a dancer. "I'd get involved in school shows," she explains, "acting or singing. Then they'd find out about my dancing and ask, 'Well, can you set up a routine for the kids?'"

Paula was happy to oblige, and before long she was staging shows on her own. "I was into choreography before I knew what it was," she says. She staged her first show, *Hello, Dolly!*, in sixth grade. It was such a hit that she went on to choreograph school productions of *Oklahoma!*, *West Side Story*, and *Seven Brides for Seven Brothers*, all before she was out of junior high!

Like her favorite performers, Paula wanted to do it all. She wanted to sing, dance, and act. She enjoyed choreographing moves for other people, but she wanted to be in front of the camera as well. She got a chance to do that in a student film called *Junior High*

Paula cooks up an experiment as a member of the Van Nuys High
science club.

School. This movie can still be seen sometimes on cable television, but Paula probably wishes it would disappear. In junior high, her nose was much more prominent than it is today, and her singing in the movie isn't exactly what you hear on her records now.

When Paula entered ninth grade, she started attending Van Nuys High, a school that lists among its graduates superstars Robert Redford and Marilyn Monroe. Paula threw herself into high school life, enjoying the same activities most teenagers do. She liked to hang out with her friends, go shopping, and see movies. But she also showed a drive and ambition that would later take her to the top of the music charts. Besides continuing her dancing lessons, she found time to play the flute in the orchestra, participate in the science club, and study hard enough to get good grades. She was a popular student and was elected May Queen and class president in her senior year.

Paula did one other thing in high school that would later make a big impact on her life—she joined the cheerleading squad. Paula didn't look like the typical cheerleader: She was short and a little bit heavy. But her enthusiasm shone through, and she soon became head cheerleader, responsible for choreographing the routines that the team would perform at basketball games.

Developing new routines gave Paula a chance to sharpen her choreography skills. "Cheerleading was so traditional," she explains, "with the pom-poms and the cheers. I felt, okay, let's do that but do some dance moves, too, so I started changing the whole style of cheerleading."

Once again, Paula used her talent to make something better, more exciting. She quickly learned how

20

Paula practices her moves as the head cheerleader at Van Nuys High.

to work with a group of dancers, and soon she was creating dynamic new routines incorporating the moves she had learned in dance class with the high-energy jazz and street moves she loved so much. "The teams were getting more involved because they really liked the dance steps," she says. It wasn't long before

Paula's routines were the star attractions at the games. Paula had proven to everyone what she already knew: that someone who didn't really fit the usual image could come out on top.

Paula did have one area of trouble during her years at Van Nuys: her unusual appearance. She has an interesting background. Her mother is French-Canadian and Jewish, and her father's heritage is Brazilian and Syrian. Because of this combination, Paula has a beautiful, exotic look that is hard to define. She also has an unusual last name. Sometimes this caused her difficulty at school when people couldn't tell if she was Hispanic, black, or white. Later, as her music career took off, she found that this interesting heritage worked to her advantage. People of all backgrounds can relate to Paula and her music.

"I feel fortunate that I'm embraced by everyone," she says, "that everyone can identify with me. Kids of all backgrounds say 'You inspire me,' and that makes me feel good."

Paula's hard work in high school paid off when in

her senior year she was offered a dance scholarship at Juilliard, the prestigious school for performing arts in New York City. But Paula had her doubts about becoming a professional dancer. "I knew I had the chops [moves]," she explains, "but I didn't have the looks. You had to be just so skinny and tall. I knew going to most auditions I probably wouldn't make it, but I just kept going. Often I wouldn't get to show off my stuff because of my shape and size. I'm a perfect example of someone who doesn't have that perfect look."

Paula turned down the Juilliard scholarship, deciding instead to enroll at the California State University at Northridge to study sportscasting. A longtime sports fan, she thought that this would be a great way for her to combine her love of sports with her dream of working in the entertainment industry. This decision would turn out to be one of the most important ones she would ever make.

2

ALL THE RIGHT MOVES

"Paula allowed me to discover things about my dancing I didn't know existed."

—Janet Jackson

Paula enjoyed her classes at Northridge. And she also kept up with her dancing, getting better and better. One day in 1982, when Paula was a sophomore, she heard that there were going to be auditions for the Laker Girls, the cheerleaders for the popular Los Angeles Lakers basketball team. Paula loved the Lakers, and she thought this would be a great opportunity to show off her dancing abilities while staying in school.

Paula went to the audition thinking that it would be just like all the other ones she had ever gone to—she'd be too short or wouldn't have the right look. When she got to the gym where the auditions were being held, her worst fears came true. There were over

◀ Paula's energy and enthusiasm are reflected in the moves that make her the hottest choreographer around.

500 other girls waiting to try out, and all of them were, as Paula says, "five feet seven with killer bodies!"

The girls were given numbers when they arrived and were auditioned when their numbers were called. Paula's number was in the 390s, and as she watched all the other girls go before her, she almost turned around and went home. Everyone seemed taller, or thinner, or prettier than she. She says, "I saw these girls and said, 'No.' I turned around and started walking out of the building."

But then she thought about all the hours she'd spent practicing and working out. She thought about all the moves she'd developed. She decided to give it her best shot.

When her turn finally came, the courageous 20-year-old exploded onto the court. She wowed the judges with a breathtaking routine that showed off her jazz, street, and classical moves in a combination that was fresh and new. The judges couldn't believe what they saw. Out of the more than 500 girls who auditioned that day, Paula was one of only 12 chosen for

26

Paula (center left) with the rest of the Laker Girls.

the new Laker Girls squad.

Paula worked hard at her new career. As a Laker Girl, she rehearsed two nights a week for about three hours at a time and did one or two games a week for $50 a game. She also continued taking her classes at Northridge.

The cheerleading routines that made up the floor shows at the Laker games offered Paula another chance to try out new moves. Once again, she was in front of an audience. She loved the energy of the crowd, and her ability and spirit were quickly noticed by the team managers. Toward the end of her first season with the Laker Girls, Paula was named assistant choreographer. After two years, she became the head choreographer.

Kristie Furuta became a Laker Girl during Paula's last year as choreographer. She remembers Paula as a dynamic choreographer whom the girls enjoyed working with. "She was a lot of fun," Kristie says. "She always came up with really interesting moves. And she was so nice. All the girls liked working with Paula. She joked around all the time. She really made my first year a lot of fun. We all miss her."

As choreographer, Paula planned all of the routines that the squad performed during their halftime shows. "I changed the whole face of cheerleading," Paula says half jokingly. "Up to then, cheerleading was shaking pom-poms, rah-rah, and beautiful girls just jumping up and down. I wanted the crowd to see some serious dancing."

Paula got rid of the pom-poms and started putting intricate dance moves into the standard routines. She used the Laker Girls floor shows to try out new styles, and it paid off. Soon the Laker Girls performances became almost as popular as the Lakers games.

At this point, Paula was spending a lot of time with the Laker Girls, and she decided to put off her studies at Northridge in order to pursue her career.

Wen Roberts, who has been the official photographer for the Los Angeles Lakers for many years, remembers Paula. "She always worked extra hard to get things just right, and people enjoyed working with her," he says. "Paula doesn't have that typical cheerleader look, but she has an incredible personality and endless energy. I always thought that she would be successful, and it's great to see her where she is today. She's a very talented lady, and one of the nicest people you'll ever meet. I still see her sometimes at sporting events, and she always takes time to say hello. Even though she's a big star, she's remained a real person."

The Lakers games also gave Paula a chance to practice her directing skills. Because the games were shown on television, she would work with the camera crew to shape the routines. She says, "Anytime a

routine was being shown I was able to work with the camera crew and tell them to get a wide-angle shot of this or that. I would have the girls work in different formations, just so the crew could get used to it and block it." This experience would later help Paula when she started making music videos to go along with her songs.

The Lakers are a world famous team, and their games draw huge audiences. Because they play in Los Angeles, this audience includes many show business people. It isn't unusual to see celebrities such as Jack Nicholson or Arsenio Hall sitting in the front row watching the games.

During one Lakers game early in the 1984-1985 season, Paula was going through a routine with the cheerleaders. To her it was just like any other night, and she put her usual energy into her performance. What she didn't know was that her moves were being watched by some members of the famous singing group The Jacksons. The Jacksons had come to see the action on the court, but instead of watching the

◀ A longtime sports fan, Paula takes a break from her busy career to attend a hockey game.

basketball players, they had their eyes on the fiery woman leading the cheerleading squad.

After the game, The Jacksons asked to meet the person who had choreographed the floor show. They were introduced to Paula. The Jacksons told her how much they liked her work with the Laker Girls. Then they gave Paula the first big break of her career. They asked her if she would choreograph some steps for their new video.

That first video, "Torture," was the start of Paula's career in show business. It earned her a Best Video of the Year nomination from both MTV and the American Video Awards. And even though she didn't win that year, she was soon flooded with requests from artists who wanted to work with her. Paula now admits that making that first video was scary. Although she had choreographed many shows, she had never worked in show business before. She says that every day she would go to the set and just make things up as she went along!

After the video for "Torture," Paula went on to

Paula leads her dancers through the funky routines that first caught the attention of The Jacksons.

choreograph the giant Victory Tour for The Jacksons. She assembled a group of dancers and taught the Jackson brothers some special moves. The Jacksons, expecially Michael, loved what she came up with. After the tour, Jermaine Jackson told a reporter, "She is in tune with street-wise dancing. I plan to work with her time and time again."

Soon after the Victory Tour, at the end of the Lakers' 1985 season, Paula was approached by the president of A&M Records. He asked her if she would be willing to choreograph a video for an up-and-coming singer A&M was trying to develop. Paula agreed.

That singer was Janet Jackson, baby sister of The Jacksons. She was about to release her third album, *Control*. Unlike her first two records, which were recorded when Janet was still in her early teens, *Control* had an electrifying dance sound. Paula was brought in to give Janet a new image, one that would fit the bold, new sound of her record.

Paula remembers that getting Janet to open up wasn't easy at first. But as the two spent more and more time together, they became very close. "I worked with her about three hours every day and got to know her," Paula says. "It took a while because she's very shy." The two women are only four years apart in age and found that they had a lot in common. Paula has been quoted as saying that Janet is "like a sister" to her.

Together, Janet and Paula created an image that reflected the sharp, sassy music of Control. Once again, Paula found her work with the Laker Girls coming in handy. "Janet wasn't a trained dancer, so we spent almost a year slowly building her a style. She loved what I'd done with the Laker Girls and a lot of those moves fit her music."

Every day Janet and Paula would go into the studio and practice in front of mirrors so Janet could watch herself move. In the end, all of their hard work paid off, and Janet's new dancing abilities were showcased in the hit video "What Have You Done for Me Lately?" When the video premiered, the world saw a new Janet Jackson. Thanks to Paula's bold moves, the timid little girl was gone and a confident new woman emerged. Janet credits a lot of her new image to Paula's teaching. "I was never quite as confident before about dancing as I am now," she says. "Paula allowed me to discover things about my dancing I didn't know existed."

Following the success of "What Have You Done for Me Lately?" Paula and Janet teamed up for three more videos. "Control," "When I Think of You," and "Nasty" were all hit videos, and each one showed off a different aspect of Paula's dancing styles. Paula even appeared in "Nasty" as one of Janet's friends. "Nasty" perfectly captured Janet's new image and was her

biggest hit. The video also won Paula the 1987 MTV Video Music Award for Best Choreography. That same year she also received the American Video Arts and Sciences Choreographer of the Year honors for her work on ZZ Top's "Velcro Fly" and was honored with an American Video Arts Award.

Working on Janet Jackson's videos was a wonderful opportunity for Paula. She learned how to direct a group of dancers and set up a scene. Most importantly, it got her noticed. After Janet's videos came out, it seemed as if everyone wanted to work with the hot new choreographer. "Working with Janet was my green card into the commercial world of choreography," Paula says. "Once her videos came out, I didn't have a day off for the next two years." Summing up her instant success, Paula says simply, "I was stunned!"

Suddenly, at the age of 24, Paula found herself constantly in demand. She helped many acts create dance numbers for their videos and live shows, working with such varied artists as the Pointer Sisters, Whitesnake, INXS, George Michael, and Duran Duran.

◀ Paula with rap star Tone Loc. As her popularity grew, Paula was in demand as a choreographer for many performers.

Because her popularity occurred so quickly, Paula still didn't have a business manager. People would look up her mother's number in the phone book and call her at home. Then Paula and Lorraine would decide how much to charge for a job!

Paula also got work in the movies, putting together a number for the movie *Dragnet*. She even taught muscle man Arnold Schwarzenegger some fancy footwork to liven up his sci-fi thriller *Running Man*!

Working in the movies fulfilled part of Paula's childhood dream of being an all-around entertainer. She had gone from watching the magic on screen to creating it. Today, she still likes to work with actors. "I give them ideas of a character to portray," she explains. "I bring out the best in them by digging it out. I like to do the feature films because you get to know the talent and grow with them to create something special."

Besides working in movies and videos, Paula managed to find time to choreograph a television Christmas special with Dolly Parton and make TV commercials for products such as Nissan cars and Michelob beer.

For two years Paula worked behind the scenes, creating hot images for other people. She enjoyed doing it. But she had always dreamed of being a star herself. She decided that it was time to come out from behind the camera. "I loved choreography," she explains, "but I wanted to be a performer. My idols were people who could do many things—sing, dance, act, choreograph." So, in 1986, Paula decided to step out from behind the camera and into the spotlight.

3

FOREVER YOUR GIRL

*"I've realized all the dreams I
ever had as a little girl."*

—Paula Abdul

Paula set her sights on making a record. There was only one problem: She had never sung professionally before!

Paula didn't let this stop her. She hired a vocal coach to help her improve her voice. Then she cut a demo—short for *demonstration*—tape. A demo tape is a tape that performers make of their songs to send to record companies. They hope the record companies will like what they hear and offer them a contract.

In the meantime, two of Paula's old friends from the music business, Jeff Ayeroff and Jordan Harris, had formed a record company called Virgin America. Jordan Harris had worked with Paula on the Janet Jackson videos, and he knew that Paula was interested in a

◀ Paula belts out one of her hit singles.

singing career. He also knew that Paula was a dynamic performer. After listening to her demo, the two men offered Paula a contract. She was one of the first acts signed to the new label.

Paula went into the studio. She worked with several producers, including L. A. Reid and Babyface, best known for producing great dance and soul music for performers like Karyn White and Pebbles, and Jesse Johnson. They were a perfect match for Paula's high-energy style.

But recording an album was not the only work Paula was doing. She was still choreographing movies, helping other singers with their tours, and choreographing the hit television comedy *The Tracey Ullman Show*. Often she would work all day and then record her album from midnight until dawn!

While she was working on the album, Virgin released a single, "Knocked Out" on a compilation album. The album featured songs by several Virgin artists, and was sent to clubs and radio stations to promote the company's upcoming records. There was

All of Paula's hard work promoting *Forever Your Girl* paid off when the album hit number one. ▶

good response, so Virgin pushed up the release date for Paula's album. After several months of hard work, Paula's first album, *Forever Your Girl*, was released in June of 1988.

At first, *Forever Your Girl* didn't do well. Despite the strong reaction to "Knocked Out," the song didn't move up the charts very quickly. It was getting played in some clubs and on black radio stations, but it wasn't a hit. Still, Paula did some live shows to support the record, singing to prerecorded tapes. Often, the crowds were very small. Once she even performed for a group of 12 Marines at a club in Hawaii.

But Paula was determined. She knew that her record was good. Virgin released another single, "The Way that You Love Me." This song, too, got some airplay on black radio, but it still wasn't the smash that Paula needed.

Frustrated, Paula almost gave up. Then, out of nowhere, dance clubs across the country started playing "Straight Up," another song from *Forever Your Girl*, and one that hadn't been released as a single.

Coincidentally, it was also the song that Paula had asked Virgin to release first, but they had ignored her.

Bold and catchy, "Straight Up" was an instant hit in dance clubs. The strong beat and unforgettable chorus made it a favorite, and soon the song jumped out of the dance clubs and onto the radio. It stormed up the charts to the number one spot, staying there for several weeks. Ironically, when her record company called her to tell her that "Straight Up" had hit number one, Paula was in bed with a fever caused by overwork. She couldn't even celebrate her hard-won success.

Suddenly *Forever Your Girl* was hot. "Knocked Out" made it into the Top 5 on the Billboard charts and was followed by "Forever Your Girl," "The Way That You Love Me," "Cold Hearted," and "Opposites Attract," all number one smashes. Music critics who had given her album poor reviews when it first came out were now describing Paula as a superstar, comparing her to Madonna and Paula's old friend Janet Jackson. Suddenly Paula was everywhere. In early 1989 she appeared as a presenter twice—at both the 16th An-

nual American Music Awards and the 31st Annual Grammy Awards.

Six months after its release, *Forever Your Girl* became the number one album in the country. It was a monster hit, selling more than 12 million copies worldwide. It stayed in the Billboard Hot 100, the list of the best-selling record albums in the country, for more than a hundred weeks, ten of them at number one. The only other debut album to achieve this was Whitney Houston's. Also, Paula's string of singles kept her in the Top 40 for 66 straight weeks, a feat equaled only by Elvis Presley, Michael Jackson, and Lionel Richie. No other woman had ever done it.

Paula had success on all the charts. Besides topping the Billboard Hot 100, she reached the top spot on the Black Top 40, the Worldwide Chart, and the Adult Contemporary Top 40. Her dream of being an all-around artist was coming true.

To accompany her singles, Paula released a string of hit videos. When people saw that behind the great voice in the songs was an even better dancer, Paula's

◄ Paula re-creates one of the hot scenes from her video for "Cold Hearted."

success skyrocketed. Her videos were in constant rotation on MTV day and night.

Besides promoting her music, the videos gave Paula the chance to pay tribute to some of her idols. In "Cold Hearted," she created a steamy dance number in the tradition of famous choreographer Bob Fosse. The video is modeled after a number from the movie *All That Jazz*, which Fosse choreographed. And in "Opposites Attract," her dancing partner is an animated cat called M. C. Skat Cat. Paula and M. C. Skat Cat dance together just like Paula's childhood idol Gene Kelly did with Jerry the dancing mouse in the film *Anchors Aweigh*. This amazing video would later win Paula a Grammy Award for Best Music Video at the 33rd Annual Grammy Awards.

For the "Straight Up" video, Paula teamed up with her longtime friend Arsenio Hall, whom she had met during her days as a Laker Girl. She also got to fulfill another wish by working with a group of children in the clip for "Forever Your Girl." One little boy in this video was so taken with Paula that he followed her

48

The young dancers from the *Forever Your Girl* video.

around all day and finally asked her for her phone number.

When asked where she gets all the great ideas for her videos, Paula says, "I wake up remembering certain things I've dreamed and dance them out in front of the mirror before my shower, while still in my pj's."

Paula also promoted her album by headlining the Club MTV Tour in the summer of 1989. Audiences around the country cheered and danced in the aisles when Paula hit the stage to the driving beat of "Straight Up" and her other hits.

The hard work and endless hours of touring and shooting videos paid off in September 1989, when Paula took home no less than four top honors at the 6th Annual MTV Video Music Awards, including Best Female Video and Best Dance Video. Less than two weeks later, she received the Best Choreography award for her work on *The Tracey Ullman Show* at the 42nd Annual Emmy Awards.

As 1990 began, Paula Abdul was on top of the charts and on top of the world. Her album was a phenomenal success, and she was a star. At the 17th Annual American Music Awards, Paula was a double winner, taking home the awards for Favorite Female Vocalist and Favorite Musical Artist. In addition, she choreographed all the dance numbers for the awards show. Later in the year she would earn her second Emmy for her work on the show. Oddly, the talented choreographer whose graceful moves won awards tripped in the aisle and fell on her way back from making her acceptance speech!

And the awards kept coming. In February, Paula

◀ Paula holds up one of the four MTV Music Video Awards she won for her work.

was a presenter at the 32nd Annual Grammy Awards, and in March, at the 16th Annual People's Choice Awards, she took home the trophy for Favorite Musical Performer.

During the summer of 1990, Paula was the recipient of another type of honor. L.A. Gear, the sportswear company, signed Paula to a $10 million deal to endorse its products. It was one of the largest celebrity contracts ever signed.

The highlight of Paula's year came when she was asked to choreograph some numbers for the 62nd Annual Academy Awards. This gave her the opportunity to combine her love of music, dance, and film. As Paula and her manager sat in the audience watching a clip of famous actresses playing behind Paula's dancers, Paula looked up at the women on the screen and whispered, "I'm going to be up there someday."

More important to Paula than all the awards and attention was the praise she received from some of her longtime heroes. After seeing her videos, Bob Fosse said that her style reminded him of his early work; and

Paula shows off some of the L.A.Gear products she will be endorsing.

choreographer Debbie Allen, one of Paula's big influences, praised Paula's fresh approach to dance. Even Gene Kelly, the man Paula used to look at for hours on screen, told reporters that he loved to watch her dance!

Paula summed up 1990 by saying, "It has been one of those years that if I was never successful again, I'd feel okay. I've realized all the dreams I ever had as a little girl."

4

SPELLBOUND

"I never had so much fun."
—Paula Abdul on making *Spellbound*

Paula started off 1991 by picking up her second People's Choice Award for Favorite Female Musical Performer. She was still on top. But now she had to decide how to follow up the success of *Forever Your Girl*. It had been almost three years since her first album, and she knew that her fans and the critics were expecting another album filled with catchy dance music.

Paula decided to surprise everyone. She announced that she wanted her next record to have a different sound. For one thing, she wanted the vocals to be richer, and she wanted the songs to showcase her voice more than the ones on *Forever Your Girl* had. To accomplish this, she hired vocal coach Gary Catona

◀ Paula wins her second People's Choice Awards for Favorite Female Musical Performer.

and spent long hours learning how to make her voice stronger.

She also surprised everyone, especially her record company, by deciding not to team up again with the same producers and songwriters who helped her achieve five smash hits. Instead, she chose to work with the Family Stand, a group of musicians and songwriters from Brooklyn, New York. The Family Stand is a funk-rock trio known for creating hard driving dance music—or house music—that is popular in clubs. Paula first heard of them when she was listening to demos of songs for her new album. After Paula listened to and rejected hundreds of songs, Gemma Corfield, an executive at Virgin, played her a tape of a Family Stand ballad called "Rush Rush." Paula knew immediately that she wanted to record the song, and asked the Family Stand if they would help her with the rest of the songs on her album.

The Family Stand agreed, and soon Paula was in the studio with the trio, laying down tracks for her new project. This time, Paula did things differently. Instead

Paula with the Family Stand, the funk-rock trio that helped her make *Spellbound*.

of relying on other people to write her lyrics and tell her how her songs should sound, she was involved in every part of putting the record together. In addition to the Family Stand, she worked with many different musicians and songwriters, including Stevie Wonder, John Hiatt, and Prince, who wrote a song called "U" especially for Paula. She also cowrote several songs, including "Will You Marry Me?," a song about a girl getting up the courage to ask a man to marry her. Asked why she wrote such an unusual song, Paula laughs. "I'm wondering if this is what I'm going to have going to have to do to get a man!"

As usual, Paula threw all of her energy into this new project. "She knew where she wanted to go," says Family Stand member V. Jeffrey Smith. "She wanted to do something different. She wanted to grow." Paula worked long hours getting her new sound just right. Amazingly, it took only four months to record her second album, *Spellbound*, about half the time it took to record *Forever Your Girl*. But if you ask Paula about all the hard work, she just laughs. "I never had so much fun."

Virgin Records gave Paula her own label, Captive Records, and released *Spellbound* on it in August 1991. Fans and critics held their breath, waiting to see if Paula had come up with something as good as *Forever Your Girl*.

Going against her record company's advice, Paula released the beautiful ballad "Rush Rush" as the first single from *Spellbound*. She admits that she was a little worried because her fans were used to hearing her sing dance music. But she wanted to show off her new voice, particularly since not long before *Spellbound*'s

A confident Paula at a press conference to promote the release of *Spellbound*. ▶

release a backup singer on *Forever Your Girl* had made claims that it was her voice heard on several of the big hits on Paula's first album. Paula held a news conference defending herself. Now her new record would prove that she could sing, and sing well.

Paula's hunch was right on target. Fans loved "Rush Rush," and the single roared up the charts and straight into the number one spot almost immediately. Radios all over the country were playing the song, and Paula could breathe a sigh of relief. She had another hit. *Spellbound* rushed into the number one spot on the Billboard album chart and stayed there for over a month. Only a few weeks after its release, the album was certified platinum, which meant it sold over one million copies.

To accompany the "Rush Rush" single, Paula made another great video. Again she surprised everyone. The video is a mini-movie. It is also another tribute, this time to the classic James Dean movie *Rebel Without a Cause*, one of Paula's favorites. In the video, which has a long acting sequence before the music begins, Paula plays a young girl in the 1950s, a part originally played by the actress Natalie Wood. She falls in love with a young rebel, played by Keanu Reeves, whom Paula met through her agent.

The "Rush Rush" video was a big risk for Paula. Because it is long, there was the danger that it might not get played on television. Most videos are about four minutes long. "Rush Rush" is over eight minutes. Also, it was a completely different Paula than her fans were used to. There were no glittery costumes or dance numbers, just Paula singing and acting.

But it was a hit. Fans loved seeing Paula act, and the video shot into the number one spot, soon becoming the most requested video on MTV. Paula's dream of becoming an all-around entertainer was coming true. She was a successful singer, choreographer, and dancer. And now she proved that she could act.

Next Paula released the hard-rocking "Promise of a New Day," a strong dance song about protecting the environment. Rather than rely on a good beat and forgettable lyrics, Paula decided to record a dance

song with a message. The accompanying video was filled with images and thoughts about protecting the world's rain forests.

The song was a big hit in dance clubs, and it, too, went straight up the charts. Paula had shown her critics that she could move from soft ballads to rockers easily. She had also proven that her first album wasn't just a lucky break. She announced to the world that she was here to stay, and that she wanted to do even bigger things. Her third release from *Spellbound*, "Blowing Kisses in the Wind," was another ballad. It, too, was a hit.

Now that her fans had gotten a chance to hear her new sound, it was time for Paula to take her show on the road. She got ready to launch a major concert tour, her first since she was part of the Club MTV Tour. Even though Paula had been in the music business for many years and knew how much work a tour involved, she was still surprised by how long it took to organize her road show. Two days before launching the Under My Spell 29-city tour, she told a *New York Times* reporter, "No one said it was going to be easy, I just didn't know

◀ Paula dazzles her audience with a song from *Spellbound*.

it was going to be this hard."

Paula was referring to the ten grueling months of work she and her tour team spent hiring a band, auditioning dancers, deciding what songs to include, building stages, rehearsing, and coming up with dazzling special effects. When the tour finally began, in October of 1991, Paula's fans were treated to a spectacular display. Movie screens played Paula's hit videos as she performed them live. She even had a real-life M. C. Skat Cat, who joined her onstage to help perform "Opposites Attract." It seemed that nothing could stop her now. Paula's hope for the future is summed up in a message she wrote to her managers, Larry Tollin and Larry Frazin, in the liner notes for *Spellbound*: "The future looks really bright, and I know that things will really be incredible from here on out."

Paula hits the stage on her first major tour. ▶

CONCLUSION: What Next?

"She makes you feel like it's possible."

—film executive Dawn Steel

On December 5, 1991, all of Paula's childhood dreams came true. She received her own star on the Holly-wood Walk of Fame. Now her star rests alongside those of Gene Kelly, Fred Astaire, and the other dancers, singers, and actors that she admired as a little girl. Like them, she has become a permanent part of Hollywood history.

That night, Paula began the first of three sold-out shows at the Great Western Forum, where she used to perform as a Laker Girl. Before the concert, former Laker Magic Johnson came onstage and announced that Paula's old cheerleading uniform was being re-tired, bringing cheers and applause from the packed

◀ A childhood dream comes true as Paula receives a star on the Hollywood Walk of Fame.

house. For Paula, it was the perfect homecoming.

The little girl who once sat on the couch watching other people dance across the TV screen has come a long way. Today she lives in a beautiful house in the Hollywood hills. She has a big pool, a spacious bedroom to hold her stuffed animal collection, and more closets than she can fill up with clothes. Her songs are all over the radio, her picture is on the cover of magazines, and she does television commercials for products such as Diet Coke.

But more important than all of that is the satisfaction Paula gets from seeing her dreams come true. She has worked hard to get where she is, and now she can look back and see what she has accomplished. She is someone many young people can look up to, for she has proven to the world that a person who doesn't fit the expected image of a cheerleader, singer, dancer, or actress can be better than all the rest if she just believes in her own ability.

What is Paula Abdul's secret? Film executive Dawn Steel says, "You can sit there in the audience and look on the screen and say, 'I can be her. I can do what she does.' She makes you feel like it's possible."

What's left for Paula Abdul to do? Well, she still does choreography, most recently creating the dance scenes for director Oliver Stone's movie about the 1960s rock group The Doors. She works for such causes as the American Red Cross and speaks out for women's rights and against drug use. She also plans to open a dance school in Los Angeles.

And she always has to think about the future. Although she is at the top now, she must work very hard to stay there. She also must deal with the fans that follow her wherever she goes. Being a celebrity means losing a lot of your personal freedom, and Paula is no exception.

Paula Abdul herself has the best explanation for her ability to stay on top. "Everyone goes through ups and downs," she says. "There are times when I feel that I just want to give up. The thing to realize is that success can happen if you stay focused and close to your heart and what you believe. Be strong and work hard to achieve your dreams. Don't give up."

INDEX

DISCOGRAPHY

Forever Your Girl
Virgin Records, 1988

Shut Up and Dance
(Remixes from *Forever Your Girl*)
Virgin Records, 1990

Spellbound
Virgin/Captive Records, 1991

VIDEO COLLECTIONS

Paula Abdul–Straight Up
Virgin Records, 1989

ABOUT THE AUTHOR

M. Thomas Ford is a children's book editor and writer. He lives in New York City, where he can frequently be seen walking his Dalmatian, Harrison, in Washington Square Park.